797,885 Books
are available to read at

Forgotten Books

www.ForgottenBooks.com

Forgotten Books' App
Available for mobile, tablet & eReader

ISBN 978-1-332-43225-7
PIBN 10426105

This book is a reproduction of an important historical work. Forgotten Books uses state-of-the-art technology to digitally reconstruct the work, preserving the original format whilst repairing imperfections present in the aged copy. In rare cases, an imperfection in the original, such as a blemish or missing page, may be replicated in our edition. We do, however, repair the vast majority of imperfections successfully; any imperfections that remain are intentionally left to preserve the state of such historical works.

Forgotten Books is a registered trademark of FB &c Ltd.
Copyright © 2017 FB &c Ltd.
FB &c Ltd, Dalton House, 60 Windsor Avenue, London, SW19 2RR.
Company number 08720141. Registered in England and Wales.

For support please visit www.forgottenbooks.com

1 MONTH OF FREE READING

at
www.ForgottenBooks.com

By purchasing this book you are eligible for one month membership to ForgottenBooks.com, giving you unlimited access to our entire collection of over 700,000 titles via our web site and mobile apps.

To claim your free month visit:
www.forgottenbooks.com/free426105

* Offer is valid for 45 days from date of purchase. Terms and conditions apply.

English
Français
Deutsche
Italiano
Español
Português

www.forgottenbooks.com

Mythology Photography **Fiction** Fishing Christianity **Art** Cooking Essays Buddhism Freemasonry Medicine **Biology** Music **Ancient Egypt** Evolution Carpentry Physics Dance Geology **Mathematics** Fitness Shakespeare **Folklore** Yoga Marketing **Confidence** Immortality Biographies Poetry **Psychology** Witchcraft Electronics Chemistry History **Law** Accounting **Philosophy** Anthropology Alchemy Drama Quantum Mechanics Atheism Sexual Health **Ancient History Entrepreneurship** Languages Sport Paleontology Needlework Islam **Metaphysics** Investment Archaeology Parenting Statistics Criminology **Motivational**

THE CONDUCT

OF THE

CERRO DE PASCO MINING COMPANY

— BY —

Dora Mayer

Manager of the Press Department

— OF THE —

"ASOCIACION PRO-INDIGENA"

LIMA..PERU
1913

THE CONDUCT

OF THE

CERRO DE PASCO MINING COMPANY

— BY —

Dora Mayer

President of the Press Committee

— OF THE —

"ASOCIACION PRO - INDIGENA"

LIMA..PERU

1913

AGREEMENT OF THE MANAGING BOARD
OF THE
ASOCIACION PRO-INDIGENA

Lima, 7 th March 1913.

Revised in to-day's session the pamphlet entitled "The conduct of the Cerro de Pasco Mining Company" written by the Press Manager of the Managing Board of the "Asociacion Pro-Indígena", Miss Dora Mayer, its contents were approved and ordered to be published.

J. CAPELO
President

PEDRO S. ZULEN
General Secretary

CONTENTS

Description of the enterprise	5
The workers	6
The economical situation of the Company	7
Payment in provisional money	8
The Mercantile	10
The discounts and the fines	11
Illegal industrialism	12
The railway-lines of the Company	13
Undermining the ground	14
The partiality of the authorities	16
The tolerance of Government	17
A "Deslinde" (demarcation of frontiers) of the estate "Paria"	18
Elections and public manifestations	20
Labour legislation	21
The labour accidents	21
The accident in the shaft "Noruega"	22
The report of Mr. Carlos A. Portella, Mining Delegate of Cerro de Pasco	24
The catastrophes in the coal-mines of Gollarisquisga	25
The Company's contempt for the workmen	26
The indemnizations	27
Other details from the Official Report (the management of the work)	28
The measures which ought to be adopted in order to avoid future accidents	29
At Congress	31
Posterior accidents	31
A typical document	36
The Cerro de Pasco Hospital	38
The Strikes	40
Latest news from Gollarisquisga and Smelter	42
Conclusion	44
Notes	48

Note.—As the printing work of this pamphlet was done by persons not familiar with the English language, the readers will please to excuse the several minor mistakes which may be found in the following pages.

The Cerro de Pasco Mining Company

DESCRIPTION OF THE ENTERPRISE

The Cerro de Pasco Mining Co. began its operations in Perú in 1901. By its magnitude, the enterprise was destined to revolutionize industrial life in this country. First of all, the primitive methods employed heretofore in the mining business, were replaced by the large modern mechanical contrivances, and in the second instance, the national property gave way to the push of the strong foreign capital, which was inverted to acquire metaliferous soil.

The North-American company spent about sixteen million dollars before it started the work of smeeting ore. Six million were invested in the purchase of mines; four in the instalment of the smelter; three in the construction of the railways to Oroya and Gollarisquisga; and finally another three in the installation of the pumps, shafts, machinery and timbering of the mines.

The first proceedings of the Company were legitimate; good prizes were offered to the owners of existing mines, inducing them by tempting propositions to transfer their possessions to the newcomer. By and bye, however, as the Company became initiated into the secrets of the judicial and political habits of the country, it made up its mind to take advantage of the frailties which unfortunately are to be found in our social system, and entered fully into the ways of fraud, bribery and violence.

We would make no remark upon this easy corruption of the businessmen who arrived here, if the Anglo-Saxon peoples did not brag so much about their moral superiority over the South-Americans and started in their diplomacy from the idea that, whilst protecting their countrymen in the exterior, they were defending the cause of civilization and morality.

No argument speaks more strongly against the Cerro de Pasco Mining Co., than its inhumane conduct towards the aboriginal workmen whom it employs in its various departments. In the following chapters we will show separately all the points on which this colossal enterprise rests, explaining at the end the theme of the accidents and culpable neglects, which is singulary serious because it proves the frightful waste of life which takes place on account of the incredible irresponsibility allowed to the managers of the business.

The Company has its works executed principally at three places: the mines of Cerro de Pasco, the smelter, where it has its head-quarter, in the vicinily of which a village has formed, known by the name of "Smelter", and the coal-mines of Gollasrisquisga.

The railway from Oroya to Cerro de Pasco, which belongs to the Company, was opened to traffic in 1904 and has a length of 82 miles; the branch to Gollarisquisga is 25 miles long and the other branches from the town of Cerro de Pasco to the mines and the smelter cover 20 miles.

The Company owns 600 lots of land at Cerro de Pasco, 300 at Gollarisquisga; other mines bought more recently at Morococha, by the line of the railway from Lima to Oroya, and the estate "Paria" at Cerro de Pasco, which measures 70,000 acres and is dedicated to the milk-industry.

In 1908, 500 men were employed on the railroad, 1600 at the works, 1000 in the silver and copper mines; 1500 in the coal-mines. Of later years we have no exact statistics.

THE WORKERS

When the Company first came to Perú, the daily wages of a miner, a class furnished almost exclusively by the aborigina race, were 30 or 45 cents for a common labourer; half a dollar or 70 cents for a pick-man and 20 cents for the boys. Some pickmen did not work for daily pay, but by contract, usually earning 7 dollars and a half for a meter of advance, which results to be one dollar or one dollar 25 cents, or a little more, uuder favourable conditions. The mining work in Perú is carried on during the night as well as the day; generally, the men earn nine days wages in the weeck, for they are able to preserve their strength whilst working 36 hours running, if they are allowed short pauses during which they chew the coca-leaf. After twelve hours rest, the labourer begins again a new round of 36 hours; without change, until the two or three months are up for which he has apparently been contracted.

The labourers are recruited amongst the inhabitants of the Andes region, who are originally peasant farmers and are brought away sometimes from long distances. The reflective reader would ask how those men can be induced to leave their small properties, which yield them their necessary support, to exchange a healthy and peaceful life with the hard and ill-paid drudgery in the mines?

Well, it is by offering them the bait of a sum of money, by way of an advance, paid under the condition that they will go to the mines and reemburse the amount by dint of their work. This method of recruiting is called the *enganche*. Sometimes the Indian is in need of money, generally because some person of a higher social standing has practised extortions on him in his native village. Some merciless creditor presses the Indian; then comes the agent of the great industrial enterprisers who are in search of labour, and places at his disposal an advance of 25, 75 or even 150 dollars, makes him sign a contract which serves as a legal instrument that obliges him to fulfil his new compromise and deprives him of his personal liberty as long as his debt to the master is not cancelled.

Means are found to prolong the subsistence of this debt much beyond its natural limits, by making discounts in the salary of the workman for fines, expenses made in the warehouses wich are annexed to the chief business and by introducing mistakes of reckoning in his weekly account-book. The case is not rare that a workman, who has been contracted for a couple of weeks, can not get away from the mine for a couple of years, or rather that, although he is allowed to visit for a short interval his native place, he must return again to work for cancelling his inxtinguishable debt, as elsewise the public authorities would arrest him wherever he be found, at the demand of the company's agents.

By raising the miserable rates of wages which then prevailed, to 1 dollar 25 cents, the Company attracted a lot of workmen, but unfortunately it did not hesitate to associate itself to the methods of exploitation we have just described, and which constitute the system of slavery for debt, wich is well familiar to those persons who in advanced countries, at in England, feel an interest in the fate of oppressed races.

THE ECONOMICAL SITUATION OF THE Company

The only revenue tax that weighs on the mining enterprises is the halfyearly contribution of 7 dollars 50 cents for each mining allotment, or *pertenencia*, as is it called, which has the dimensions of a rectangle of 200 by 100 metres. (*)

In 1890 a law was given, under the influence of a mistaken idea of the necessity of extraordinarily pushing the mining industry, which was too generous and prescribed that before 1915 no new tax could be laid on the said industry, nor the exportation of its products. Moreover, the importation of machinery, as of other accesories and tools, is exempt of custom-house duties, and also coal, wood, dinamite, quicksilver and all material used in the construction and exploitation of railways.

After the large expenses attending the installation of the Cerro de Pasco Company's works, the returns in copper from its

(*) *See note A*

mines amounted already in 1906 to 15,000 per annum. The new improvements made in the smelter in 1908, caused this, marvellous power of production to be duplicated, it being calculated that it, will rise to 50,000 tons a year.

The coal mines of Gollarisquisga, which provide Cerro de Pasco with fuel, yielded 500 tons of coal daily in 1906 and their product had risen already in 1908 to 800 tons daily.

Such is the enormous benefit realized by the North-American Company of the Cerro de Pasco, almost undiminished by any charge of whatever kind. Added the fabulous cheapness of labour to the privileges which the laws of the country award to the mining business, one would believe that those advantages were sufficient to satisfy the ambition of the most greedy business-man. However, a human being who has once entered the course of shameless profit will not be content even with an excess of gain.

PAYMENT IN PROVISIONAL MONEY

Whenever the work of poor people is retributed, it ought to be done at short intervals, because thus it behoves with regard to the insufficient administrating capacity and the narrow economical situation of the humble classes. For this reason the payment of wages to the workmen of factories and other similar industries is effected generally every week, or at most, every fortnight. At the smelter of Cerro de Pasco this rule is not observed, for the payment in ready money is made every 10 th of the month. Every afternoon when leaving his work, the labourer receives a metal coin, which he must exchange in the morning for one of cardboard, which the head-man gives him, filling in the name of the receiver and short annotations regarding his services. After having earned several of these pieces of cardboard the possessor can go and change them at the cashier's for a bond which enables him to purchase articles at the Mercantile, where it is accepted because this establishment is a dependency of the Company. Oftentimes the Indians fail to understand this arrangement at the beginning and keep the metal coins without exchanging them for the pieces of cardboard, thus losing their pay. The bond issued one week does not keep valid for the next, so that the period of its usefulness is limited (the reader mark what an ingenious system of exploitation this implies.)

This question of paying in provisional money has no justification in the present concrete case, because Cerro de Pasco lies at a short distance from the capital, being connected with it directly by rail, so that the funds for entertaining the work can be remitted there with all regularity. The measure of paying the workmen in provisional money had its origin in those industrial and agricultural centres which were established in places very far away from civilization, so that the cash could not always be forwarded there for the right terms.

Notwithstanding the reasons which could be urged in favour of the use of provisional money, the same was prohibited by law, as early as 1879, in consideration of its pernicious effects upon the welfare of the working class. The aforesaid law resulted to be no hindrance, though, to the illegitimate continuance of the former custom, which was tenaciously upheld in the face of reiterated protest raised in the Senate by Dr. Joaquin Capelo, whose appeals were seconded occasionally by a few other public representatives. (*)

Dr Capelo, an energetic speaker, said in the session held by his Chamber on 24th August 1911, that it was already the fourth time he touched upon the same subject, without having obtained so far that Government should make effectual its authority in the matter. He called to mind examples regarding the Tramway Company of Lima, which issued at one period rubber coins, and of a similar company at Trujillo, as also of various agricultural companies in the North, which had been obliged by Government to retire from circulation their illegal money equivalents. "What happens", asked the speaker, "with the Cerro de Pasco Mining Co, that it does not retract its abuse, after the repeated denouncements which have been made?" Do we gain anything by the fact that a powerful Company is allowed to reduce to nothing the life of millions of citizens, ruining their families and giving them wages which are insufficient to keep them fed? All these methods which I have long ago demanded that should disappear, are permitted instead to grow day by day, and the monopoly of the merchadise is also increasing. And not only that, but contributions have been put on the merchandise, and created in the name of schools, hospitals, etc. and measures have been adopted which it would take an authorized government to introduce. That place seems like an independent nation; it forms a state; it is not North America that rules there; I rather would it were, for if the laws of the United of States were made effective in the domains of the Cerro de Pasco Mining Co., I am sure that the attentates which are committed there daily against the life and property of the residents, would find no support."

In the account of the session of the Chamber of Deputies of the same year, appears the following demand of Mr. Martinez: "That a note be passed to the respective minister, asking him to issue orders tending to prohibit in the mining district of Cerro de Pasco the use of provisional money or paper equivalents for the payment of wages to the workmen, in obedience of the prescript contained in art. 11 of the by-law for labour-contracts in the mining business, promulgated by supreme resolution of 4th September 1903, the same not being admitted either as payment given by anticipation, nor upon account and it being declared that the payment must be executed m ready money, under waning of; punishment for the infractors and the public authorities who omit to give their support to the complainants."

The first motion, demanding the suppression of provisional money in Cerro de Pasco, was made by instigation of Dr. Capelo in the Senatorial Chamber, in the month of November 1909. The

---

(*) see Note B.

last result regarding this affair, of which we have knowledge is a supreme resolution of 27 th December 1911, which provides that:

« 1. The Cerro de Pasco Mining Co shall withdraw from circulation, within three days, the bonds or warrants which it has issued and abstain in the future from issuing such documents or analogous ones.»

« 2 The prefecture of Junin shall dictate efficient measnres in order to assure the exact fulfilment of this resolution and inflict the respective punishment in case of disobedience.»

In February 1912 it was affirmed that Mr Pedro Larrañaga had accomplished at Cerro de Pasco the official commission of recollecting all the bonds of the kind which the Company delivers to its workmen.

More than two years of struggle had it cost to convert into a practical reality a láw given by the State and shamelessly infringed by the autocratic wilfulness of a private company! And who will guarantee that the cherished bonds of the speculators of Cerro de Pasco may not reapper as soon as Mr. Larrañaga turns his back?

It is really impossible to understand why the Peruvian Government is so tolerant with the arbitrarities of the North-American Company, moreover when taking into account that the gigantie enterprise leaves hardly any benefit for the state.

THE MERCANTILE

This is name which carries the famous storehouse of the Company. Almost all the wares which it sells are imported from the United States, and the prizes it asks are often 30 % higher than those current in other stores of the place. The workers of the foundry are obliged to make their purchases there, because they have no real money in hand, but only the bonds which are not accepted elsewere. This system of exploitation would even yet be a little less cruel without the further restriction of declaring the bonds valid only for a week, so that at the end of the term the Indians are induced to buy articles they do not want, so as not to lose altogether the quantity represented by the note.

Cerro de Pascó is situated in a province where the breeding of cattle is greatly developed, and meat is relatively cheap and of regular quality. Vegetables can be obtained during the principal part of the year in great variety from the neighbouring regions of Tarma and Concepción, not to mention the products from the Lima market; notwithstanding these advantageous conditions, the mining population is condemned to suffer privation in the midst of abundance; owing exclusively to the monopoly exercised by the North-American mining enterprise.

An Englishman who had been staying for some time at the Smelter, wrote to a Lima newspaper: "In the large industrial centres in Europe, which are situated apart from inhabited places, the companies themselves establish well-stocked warehouses, which furnish the labourers with every necessary at equitable prizes. Here, at Cerro de Pasco it is a perfect hipocrisy of the Company to pretend that it has founded the Mercantile as a benefit for its men."

According to the same informant, the service at the hospital is deficient for the superior employées of the Company, and it is easy to imagine how much more so it will be for the humbler dependents of the establishment. Every employée contributes in proportion to his salary from 25 cents upwards to 1 dollar to the funds of the hospital, where notwithstanding, very frequently, the most ordinary remedies are wanting. The common labourer's tribute is 1 dollar monthly.

THE DISCOUNTS AND THE FINES.

It is a general rule in Perú, authorized by an evil routine' that the daily wages of contracted workmen suffer a discount of 10 cets, which go to pay the commission to the recruiting agent. Thus every labourer yields a fine rent to the contractor during the month he remains at work. Furthermore, a sum is deducted from the wages for the purpose of reembursing the advance which has been given by the agent to the labourer. The rest of the salary is sure to be grasped by the storekeeper who has furnished his victim at scandalous prizes with the articles indispensable for life, and not that even is enough, because the speculators, besides consuming all the poor man's income, will still annote in his accountbook a large sum for debt.

In case the contracted labourer should take to flight, he would be taken, and would then, for punishment, have to work gratis up to the value of 70 % of the advance he had received, 20 % being reckoned as a fine and 50 % as an indemnization for the expenses of the persecution.

Any day, besides, the labourer may find his wages diminished by the fines which the foremen impose by their own sovereign caprice. As this point is subject to no rule whatever and leaves a nice income for the employées, besides prolonging the labourer's state of insolvence, advantage is taken of it as of a lucrative business.

It is easy to invent certain delinquencies, like for instance, disrespect to the superiors, and there have even been cases, like that of the Indian Fidel Villayzán, which was denounced by the "Minero Ilustrado" of Cerro de Pasco of 12 th October 1910, on whom a fine of 5 dollars was imposed, expressly for the reason of having presented himself with a (just) complaint against the Company, before the political authority of the province.

The above-named periodical says in the same edition, that the superintendent of the Company had invested himself with the character of vice-consul of the United States in order to gain more prestige and be able to wave the official summons urging him to attend to the claims of the workmen.

ILLEGAL INDUSTRIALISM

In its zeal of monopoly, the Cerro de Pasco Mining Co is loth to permit any commercial activity besides its own, in the region where it operates.

The transport of the metals from Cerro de Pasco to the port of Callao is effected on the Company's railway-lines as far as the Andine station of Oroya, and from there on the trains of the Peruvian Corporation, which run since 1893. By its powerful influences, the Company has obtained a privilege for the transportation of its products and merchandise on the trains of the English enterprise, which simply means the exclusion or postergation of the rest of the commerce of that region. The railway-material of the Peruvian Corporation is hardly sufficient to uphold the commercial movement of the Cerro de Pasco Co, and meanwhile, the articles consigned to the markets of the Andes cities remain packed in the Lima stations, whilst at the opposite extreme, the export-articles from the mountain-places cannot get to the coast.

On occasion of a big earth-slip which happened on the Oroya line, at a place called Chaupichaca, at the beginning of 1909, traffic was congested to a degree, that with the preference given to the Cerro de Pasco Co, the town of Tarma, capital of the province of the same name, was exposed to famine, for want of the arrival of supplies from Lima.

The newspapers then raised a clamour before Government, demanding that the Peruvian Corporation should be obliged to serve the general interest, without making perilous distinctions. The several private mining enterprises of Yauli and Morococha, which enjoyed no preference, had to stop their work, and the markets of the smaller centres of labour remained deprived of all essential elements, when, upon the traffic being reopened, the great companies of Cerro de Pasco and Casapalca, supplied themselves within a fortnight of all necessaries and daily received whole trains laden not only with victuals, but also coal, wood, machinery etc.

At ordinary times these abuses are repeated in a manner just as mortifying, although perhaps a little less serious. Several mining enterprises which had managed to subsist in the beginning at the side of the properties acquired by the Cerro de Pasco Mining Co., were obliged to suspend their labours because of the indirect hostility they had to bear from the Oroya Railway, which purposely retarded the conduction of minerals destined for the Casapalca smelter or for Europe, in order to kill the minor industry.

The Company in its desire to hinder all commerce besides its own, has gone to the extreme of monopolizing the two essential elements of life, water and salt; it does not monopolize the air because it cannot. The North-American Company did not rest till it became the expenditor of water for the population of Cerro de Pasco; being clever enough to subordinate the distribution of this useful liquid, in the same way as other things, to the play of its interests. For the sale of salt it celebrated a contract with the society that administers the salt which is placed under the monopoly of the State; causing the scarcety of this article at the general market of the place.

THE RAILWAY-LINES OF THE COMPANY.

It might be expected that a North-American company would set the example of regularity and tidyness in its railway-service. However we shall see what shape has taken from the very beginning the progress which the Cerro de Pasco Mining Co. pretended to have introduced in Perú. We extract the following data from a number of " El Eco de Junin " of October 1908.

" Neither at the branch-lines from Cerro de Pasco to Smelter, nor to Gollarisquisga, are the trains subject to a fixed itinerary in their voyages to and fro, nor do they have the reglamentary kind of carriages for the passengers, as the Railway Ordinance requires."

According to the decree issued by the Office of Public Works, which was published in 1907, the trains which run on the lines of Gollarisquisga and Smelter were allowed to admit passengers in the car called the "cabouse", at second class tariff, that is to say, 75 cents per ticket, until the Company should be able to put at the disposal of the public the reglamentary carriages.

A year after this decree, the Company, taking advantage of the endurance of the public, continued to use this "cabouse", though no longer as a second-class, but as a first-class carriage, asking the prize of 1 dollar 50 cents for the ticket to Gollarisquisga and 40 cents to Smelter.

By way of second-class carriage, a car was added that deserved no better name than that of a hog-sty, in which the workmen were huddled together in utter dirtyness and almost without any light. This train of modern style vanquished the distance of 52 kilómetres, which separates Cerro de Pasco from Gollarisquisga, in 7 or 8 hours generally, although an old diligence of the XVIII century would probably have been able to do so in 4 or 5 hours. Upon one occasion, the train which left Gollarisquisga at midday, reached Cerro de Pasco at 3.0 clock in the morning, the delay being attributable to the accidents consequent upon the circumstance that the engine had to drag 28 or 30 cargo ears over almost circular curves, with evident disregard for the security of the living beings it conducted. In this train came a wounded man and another, sick with typhus fever, from Gollarisquisga. The icy wind of those heights whistled through the broken window-panes of the cabouse, the so-called first-class carriage. For certain families whom the Company distinguishes and to whom it facilitates opportunities to go to "surprise-parties", there are decent carriages which are dispatched at any hour of the day or night, and to any place whatever, whilst the workmen who bring forth the copper for the North-American commerce and in a body pay 350 dollars for hospital-dues, have to travel, when sick, without receiving food nor assistance, in a train which crawls miserably to its place of destination in perhaps 12 hours time.

With reference to those facts the local press reminded the North-American Company of the principles which are established in the United States regarding the railway service and the duties to be fulfilled towards the public.

UNDERMINING THE GROUND

The reckless manner in which the Company carries on the underground work, implies no doubt the most serious disconsideration against the neighbourhood in which it is settled. To such a degree have the necessary works of support been neglected in the mines, that the principal quarters of the town of Cerro de Pasco are in danger of ruin.

We read in a number of the "Eco de Junín" of May 1909: "The regions of "Peña Blanca" and "Noruega"; the streets of Marquez, Lima, Santa Rosa, Piura, Cajamarca, Huancavelica and Huancayo, are in imminent danger of disappearing. Most of the buildings situated in those places show considerable rents and so does the surface of the ground; many inhabitants have abandoned their homes to avoid being the victims of a tragic and violent death. Near the mine of "Peregrina" a cottage has already fallen down, burying two poor men under its ruins. Two houses, which belong to Mr. Ceferino Malpartida and Mr. Cosme Gallo, respectively, and lie in the inmediate neighbourhood of the aforesaid cottage, threaten to fall down and have been abandoned by their inhabitants. We know that the owners have presented themselves to the Cerro de Pasco Mining Co. to make claims for the loss of their property and that the reply given by the managers of the sindicate was "why had they built upon their mines?"

Not once in the period before the arrival of the North-Americans, when already hundreds of mines were being worked, did one single case of destruction happen in the city, because the miners took care not to excavate the upper parts of the ground on which the buildings rested. (*)

The principal galleries of the mines of Cerro de Pasco, which attain to the length of 1,300 metres, are well worked, illumined by electric light and protected by wooden supports of 12 by 12 inches wide, imported from the States. These works are shown to the tourists, who spread abroad the fame of the colossal North-American undertaking, but not so the branch-works, in which the gangs of miners penetrate at the risk of being buried alive.

The lowest level reached in the mines of Cerro de Pasco is over 400 feet.

(*) See note C.

In August 1911, the Company presented to the Peruvian government a project for removing the town of Cerro de Pasco to a site distant from the mines, pretending to offer for the purpose a tract of ground, which however, was not its own, and moreover wholly uneven and unhealthy, as trustworthy informants assure us.

There is no reason indeed why the landowners who hold properties in the zone which is menaced by the mining works, should lose the value of their lots of ground simply on behalf of a company which tries every means to expulse them from the locality without paying them an equitable indemnization.

A number of inhabitants of Cerro de Pasco built in these latter years a new settlement, called "Alto Perú", made up of a population of 600 persons more or less, in the vicinity of the village of "Smelter", which formed around the big establishment of the North-Americans. The Company immediately grew alarmed, thinking that the merchants of Alto Perú would make a considerable competition to its warehouse, the "Mercantile", and resolved to isolate this settlement from their own dependencies, by erecting a wall between the two, of 8 feet in height, totally closed in all its extent and with a deep moat at its bottom, which would effectually impede any access in that direction. Besides the wall, a high wire fence with points was run all round the village of Smelter, the indispensable outlets being severely guarded, so that not an employee or workman of the Mining Co., of whom there are more than 2000, could buy a cent of bread at Alto Perú.

The just-named Alto Perú is a settlement which has been spontaneously founded to replace the town of Cerro de Pasco, condemned to be reduced to ruin sooner or later by the mining works. This effort of a few thrifty employées of the Company has to be stifled, because it is the purpose of the North-Americans to reemburse all the money spent in salaries to the workmen, by dint of obliging them to buy all articles necessary for their subsistence within the iron circle it has drawn around them. The Company will take pride in being able to say some day, when it returns to the United States, laden with the fabulous treasures of the Cerro de Pasco, that it did not leave a cent in the country to whom it owes its fortune. All that it leaves behind will be ruin, desolation, misery and the remembrance of ill-treatment.

Another point that must be mentioned is the danger of the explosives to which the Company recklessly exposes the neighbourhood.

In September 1909, for instance, a deposit of dinamit was established at a place called Yanacancha, near the shaft Diamante.

Yanacancha is simply a part of the town of Cerro de Pasco, where stands the church of the same name - and many old houses are to be seen, besides a new quarter in the direction of the road to Huánuco, where at that period several buildings were being raised, and the whole area was altogether wellpeopled, not counting the labourers and employées working at "Diamante", whose number would amount to about 200 persons.

Notwithstanding the means of security that might have been adopted at the installation of this deposit, the menace to the whole town was imminent, of which not a stone would have been left upon the other in the case of an explosion. The possibility that one of the electric discharges, which are so frequent in mountain places, might blow up the dinamite, makes it urgent indeed that such deposits should be removed anyhow at four or five kilometres' distance from Cerro de Pasco.

THE PARTIALITY OF THE AUTHORITIES

Evidently, the Company must have the acquiescence of the local authorities, even before that of the central government, if it wants to reach its object of accommodating the whole social order to its own convenience. In fact it has gained for its cause the members of the town-council, the subprefects, judges and mining delegates, that is to say, all those functionaries who ought to make the people's and the State's interest weigh in the balance against that of the industrial powers. It might be argued that under the circumstances, the above-named factors being subjected by influences opposed to the honest exercise of their respective duties, the supreme government was deprived of those fountains of information upon which it had a right to rely if it were not that the frequent denouncements made in the press and other places, kept it continually aware of the misbehaviour of the Company.

In 1908, several lawsuits were pending between the Company and the municipality of Cerro de Pasco, which were near being solved favourably to the interests of the people. Thus it was urgent that at the municipal elections the list of candidates who promised to be subservient to the Company, should win, and whatever employee or workman dared to vote in a contrary sense, was abruptly and brutally destituted from his place.

The "Minero Ilustrado", N. 762, recalls to memory the violent form in which the Company began its proceedings at Cerro de Pasco, breaking the door which communicated the section of "Carrizal" with the drain of Quinlacocha, in order to obstruct the mines, so that they might become attainable at a low price; the unwarrented manner in which it started lawsuits so as to despoil the owners of their mining properties, as for example in the case of the mines "Dolores de Ijurra" and "Grande del Rey"; the mistification brought to bear upon legal proofs, which were separated from the documents they belonged to and thus used as testimonies before the tribunals, whose sentences could by this device be made to favour the Company, with great damage to the plaintiffs.

Never was the Company worse represented, by a young

man of the name of Joseph Flemming, than at the period at which the "Minero Ilustrado" makes the foregoing remarks, nor worse advised than by the unscrupulous lawyer Carlos Gómez Sanchez.

The partiality of the judges was fully evidenced in the case of the death of the unfortunate labourer Heriberto Mansilla, who was made a victim of the alcoholic fury of two North-Americans, a crime which the parties concerned intended to leave unpunished. Mansilla was ill-treated, for an insignificant reason, in a way that left him dead on the spot, in the presence of many witnesses, yet notwithstanding, the Company obtained that the only one of the two culprits who was caught, Thomas A. Barton, should enjoy an order of release, issued by the judge of peace, Bernardo Cueto, in the very face of the medical certificate of Dr. Valentine, which proved the homicide.

A few years before, a similar case occurred, the culprit being young Mr. M'Kune, the son of the first negotiator of the Cerro de Pasco mining enterprise, who, of course, escaped from justice.

On the other hand, whilst criminal cases are waved in this arbitrary manner, the prisons of the province are full of poor Indians, accused of small thefts, who expiate in utter abandonment, for indefinite periods, their real or imaginary faults.

THE TOLERANCE OF GOVERNMENT

The deference shown by our Government towards the Cerro de Pasco Mining Co., which is hard to understand, is rendered, no doubt to the North-American nationality of that enterprise.

Attention might be called towards the fact, that the powerful capitals which emigrate from the United States and other countries of like importance, destined to be employed in virgin regions, become emancipated from discipline altogether, because they are not subjected any more either to the laws of their own country nor to those of the new place of residence. A company like that of Cerro de Pasco, claims to be North-American in order to make demands against some conditions which affect its interests in the Latin-American society, but it owns to no North-American citizenship in the sense of obeying the rules which within the precincts of the fatherland would modify its conduct.

The Cerro de Pasco Co., just the same as many similar institutions, is not of North-American nationality so far as to observe those considerations towards the workmen, as would be natural in the home of Grant and Sherman, nor to keep neutrality as it ought to have done in the attempt of revolution of 1909, when it interfered actively on behalf of one of the fighting parties, no matter whether it was for the government or the rebel side.

This is perhaps the first time that, by a clear exposition

of the attitude which the foreign capital takes in South-America, the judgment of North-American and European statesmen may be altered with regard to the credit they always have given to their own countrymen. Whilst it is difficult to find an example where diplomatic action has been zealous in calling to order the agents of a foreign business established in our territory, the number of those abound, where exaggerated pretensions of such speculators have been officially supported from abroad. Can there be rights without obligations? Can this one-sided attitude of the European and North-American diplomacy be accepted as just?

Supposing that a foreigner should identify himself with the backward state of the country into which he immigrates and accommodate himself to its imperfections to the degree of turning a slaveholder and political intriguer, without attempting in the least to propagate the higher culture of his own race, what civil category ought he to occupy? Does he appear to be a son of the country of his residence or of his origin? If the former is the case, his native country should not protect him; if the latter, let him be obliged to observe a correct conduct.

Of course, the governments of weak countries will fain have to render the most abject homage to the arbiters of their destiny, whilst companies, which possess no other merit before their own country than having ammassed big fortunes by illegitimate means, are allowed to move the diplomatic resorts of the Powers.

We invite the other republics of the Latin continent, who have suffered so much from diplomatic interventions, to present their suit in the same fashion as ourselves, to the state offices, and tribunals of public opinion in Europe and North-America; so, as to form the South-American defence in such kind of cases.

A "DESLINDE" (DEMARCATION OF FRONTIERS) OF THE ESTATE "PARIA"

A circumstance which causes great evils in a country like Perú, and which appears strange in societies that are older and therefore better ordered, is that the limits of the landed property are not well defined. The owners of adjoining land-properties are almost always in dispute about stretches of territory which each of them considers to be his, until at last, one of the parties, or all of them, by common assent, ask for a judicial action, called the «deslinde», at which the judge decides the demarcation of limits, according to the title-deeds and proofs presented to him, upon the very ground in dispute, accompanied by the litigants and their advocates.

On occasion of these "deslindes" often ensue violent collisions between the opposite parties amongst themselves or against the authorities, because the anxiousness of the land-owners on one hand to extend as much as possible their propierties, and the scant scrupulosity of judges and lawyers on the other, make the affair, a matter of intrigues which incite the passions of those interested in it

It being a fact that the foreigners, when once they adopt the faults current in the country, do so to a superlative degree, the North-American Company showed that it was no exception to this rule when it endeavoured to appropriate the whole town of Cerro de Pasco, by dint of extending unduly the natural limits of an estate, called "Paria", which it had purchased in the vicinity of the place. In order to put a stop to the furtive advances of the Company, the Town Council of Cerro de Pasco required the judicial operation of the "deslinde" to be practised, and obtained, notwithstanding the resistence and evasion offered by its adversary, that the act should take place, under the auspices of the honest judge, Doctor Blondet, on Wednesday October 21 st 1908. The Company brought forward, in support of its plea, a document dated in the year 1798 in which the Convent of Nazarene Nuns alleged that a part of the community of Cerro de Pasco and some portions of land considered as belonging to other properties, were comprehended in the rightful area of the estate "Paria". These same documents named however, those places in detail, as having been possessed, even as early as 1798, for immemorial time by the miners of Cerro de Pasco, and expressed that the said Convent of the Nazarenes had no intention of despoiling the present owners of their property thus consecrated by secular tradition. Consequently, the Municipality of Cerro de Pasco, which energetically defended in this process the rights of the citizens, found excellent means to win the battle against the Cerro de Pasco Mining Company, which thought little of swallowing a whole town of Perú by one gulp.

The act of the "deslinde" of the Paria Estate was effected at ten o'clock in the morning of the day already mentioned, in the presence of the Judge, Dr. Oscar Blondet, the advocates of the Town Council, Drs. Avelino Ochoa and Raúl Noriega, the Major, Mr Juan Azalia, the Recorders, Messrs. Antonio Biasevich and Hilario P. Porras, the Lieutenant-Major, Dr. Verástegui, the advocates of the Cerro de Pasco Mining Company, Drs. Carlos Gomez Sanchez and Francisco Garcia Jimenez, the representatives of the same, Messrs. Maclennan, Flemming and Stone, and a riding party composed of more than a hundred citizens of the district.

After the explanations made by the lawyers and the presentation of the title deeds, the judicial retinue went over the entire zone of the disputed territories around the town. The ceremony ended at 1 p. m. and during its course the people of Cerro de Pasco, who witnessed it, behaved like a model of morality and order.

At the time, the defenders of the rights of the town of Cerro de Pasco seem to have ignored the strongest and most incontrovertible title which existed in their favour, namely a document guarded in the National Archive, attesting that by Royal Warrant Cerro de Pasco was erected into a mining place and the necessary area conceded by the Crown for the building of a town.

ELECTIONS AND PUBLIC MANIFESTATIONS.

The North-American Company considers its workmen as slaves, in all cases except one: when the opportunity arrives to present them as voters in its favour at the municipal elections or as partakers in some public manifestation. Then it forgets that the Indians are illiterate and so contemptible that they deserve no beds to sleep in nor pensions to relieve their situation when misfortune has befallen them, and appears to uphold that its men are able citizens, and free beings, who have decided to render a public testimony of sympathy to their chiefs.

We have in our possession the copy of a telegram which the Major of Cerro de Pasco, Mr. Juan Azalia, addressed to the Director of Government, on 31st October 1908 when the municipal elections were in course of proceeding. It runs as follows:

To the Director of Government. Lima

Yesterday, the Board of Register was grossly insulted by a mob of workmen intentionally made drunken by the American Company, under the leadership of its lawyer, Carlos Gomez Sanchez, who paraded through the streets, pronouncing invectives against the Town Concil and hurrahs for the Prefect.

I have just sent an official letter to the Sub-Prefect, requiring the help of the police for the purpose of maintaining order. The Town-Council and citizens of Cerro de Pasco, ask Government for ample protection.

AZALIA Major.

In a few words is depicted the situation which was created for the pacific citizens of Cerro de Pasco by the ambition of the Mining Company to exercise a powerful influence within the body of the new Municipality. The Prefect had been won over to its cause; and a few bad Peruvian elements were organizing an agitation in its favour, and preparing a revolt which attained to bloody extremes, with the indirect applause of the Norh-American managers.

Similar scenes were provoked shortly before upon occasion of the act of demarcation of limits of the estate "Paria", which we have described in the preceding chapter. The Major, Mr. Azalia, sent at that time the following official letter to the Prefect of the Department of Junin:

A seal of the Major's Office.

Cerro de Pasco, October 20th 1908.

To the Prefect of the Department.

Mr. Prefect:

At this Major's Office has been received intelligence that the Cerro de Pasco Mining Company prepares a numerous troupe of employeés and workmen in its service, with the purpose of making them concur armed, at the act of the demarcation of limits between this town and the estate "Paria", property of the Company.

This measure can only be deemed an act of direct provocation towards the citizens who are interested in the demarcation affair and therefore I have the honour to appeal to Your Honour, that Your Honour may dictate the most efficient orders to avoid any conflict and preserve the public peace.

God preserve Your Honour.

JUAN AZALIA

It was rumoured that at Smelter the Americans held ready a protected car, destined to execute the warfaring operations intended to be realized on occasion of the "deslinde".

Two days before the ceremony circulated the news that the superintendent of the Cerro de Pasco Mining Company had issued a general order at the carpenter's shop to make 500 cudgels, with which to arm a legion of employees and workmen who were to meet at the "deslinde". It was remembered, upon this occasion, that the same measure was employed at Morococha, in 1906, when the wealthy miner, Mr. Lizardo Proaño, was to be despoiled of the San Miguel mine, until then his property.

In view of the startling irregularities which happened at Cerro de Pasco. the Government was obliged to send a special commissioner, Mr. Manuel A. Maurtua, to the place, in order to investigate personally the causes of public disconcert revealed by the communications received.

LABOUR LEGISLATION

The law of responsibility for labour accidents, in force at present, was proclaimed on January 20 th 1911. Although much is wanting here to make labour legislation complete, the principle of the master's responsibility for the security of his employees is established in this law, in strict accordance with the theories of modern science upon the subject; the amount of the indemnizations in cases of accident is fixed therin, the same as the means of precaution which must be adopted to guarantee the life and health of the underlings and the judicial proceedings which shall help the claimants, to obtain their rights.

Under these conditions may be judged the attitude which the Cerro de Pasco Company has observed regarding the cases of accidents which have happened in its mining and smelting departments.

THE LABOUR ACCIDENTS.

The "Minero Ilustrado" of Cerro de Pasco, a paper which we have already mentioned several times in the course of this review, says in its number of July 19 th 1911, that the victims of accidents amongst the Company's labourers amount to a thousand, besides those killed in the horrible hecatombs of Gollarisquisga, which repeated themselves at short intervals during the year 1910, that is to say, in the months of January, August, September and October.

When the railway between Oroya and Cerro de Pasco was near being finished, an explosion of dinamite occurred, which cost the lives of a whole gang of workmen.

As the space and character of this publication do not allow of a too minute and technical specification of details, we will only add, by way of example, a document related with the misfortune which happened at the shaft "Noruega" on 16 th december 1908, an extract from the Record to Government by the Mining Delegate of the district of Cerro de Pasco, Mr. Carlos A. Portella, and another extract of a report which was formulated after the second catastrophe at Gollarisquisga, by a special commission named by the Minister of Public Works and the Corps of Mining Engineers, with the object of investigating the facts and propose the necessary measures to avoid the repetition of such accidents, composed by Messrs. Edmundo N. Habich, Director of Public Works, José I. Bravo, Director of the Corps of, Mining Engineers and Carlos A. Portella, Mining Delegate of Cerro de Pasco, as Secretary.

The number of 29 killed and 56 wounded was confessed after the first catastrophe of Gollarisquisga, although it must be adverted, that neither the Company, nor any person of authority had the least interest in drawing up exact statistics of the mortality of the workmen,

The magnitude and frequency of the accidents which happened at that period in the coal-mines of Gollarisquisga, aroused the public from its habitual indolence and created sensation in all social spheres. It is by this reason that some important documents were produced and published, under the passing influence of humanitarian emotions, which soon were blotted out; however, in the turmoil of egoistical sruggles.

THE ACCIDENT IN THE SHAFT "NORUEGA"

This event happened on 16 th November 1908 in the following manner: Seven workmen, called Pedro Lopez, Genaro Paucar, Guillermo Viso, Justo Perez, Santos Guzmán, Lino Yupanqui, and Marcos Hidalgo were raised to the surface, after their nights' work in order to return to their homes. They were already nearing the mouth of the shaft, and their lungs were just receiving the first breath of pure air, when the conductor of the winch, with inconceivable temerity, suddenly left loose the handle of the brake, so that the cage, going with full velocity, struck against the car occupied by the seven men, of whom five were thrown out through the shock and two remained hanging on to the car, as by a miracle, being saved from destruction.

The act of the engine-driver called Valverde, could only be explained if he was in a state of somnolence, it being 20 minutes, past 5 in the morning when the misfortune happened, or in a state of nervous agitation, owing to the circumstance of his handling two cages at the same time with different motors. Regarding both these contingencies it is necessary to make a very serious observation.

The engine-driver was not so much to be blamed for the accident, so said the witnesses, as the head-men of the Company, who, in obedience to a spirit of ill–advised economy, had establishid in some shafts the practice of letting one man manage two winding engines at the same time, with the purpose of extracting considerable quantities of metal without paying nore than one man's wages. A professoinal authority tells us, that this point is hard to understand, for it seems to be a technical absurdity to suppose that one man should handle simultaneously two motors and two drums for unrolling the cable, whereas on the other hand, the up and down cage is always attended to by a single individual. Since, however, the Mining Delegate censures in an official document the proceeding employed, we must believe that the first-mentioued,, technical absurdity is referred to.

Another consideration is the following: the foremen of a shaft do not display the necessary energy to oblige the engine drivers to attend to their work at the due hours and at ther right turn, so that it happens often that the man who is at work finds himself obliged to continue, because he is not relieved, for **16 and 32 hours**, instead of **8 hours**, which legimately correspond to him, it being quite natural that the excessive strain should produce in him sleepiness and fatigue, which would bring about the danger of his causing unintentionally the death of the workmen. The record addressed by the Commissioner to the Mining Delegation bears testimony that Valverde was not drunk, that he neither knew who went in the car and that he had practice in managing the winch.

Upon occasion of this accident, the Mining Delegation issued the following edict:

Cerro, 17 th December 1908

"In view of the account registered on the preceding page, and it being the duty of this Delegation to watch over the security of the workmen, and in the exercise of the attributions conceded by the ordinance about the mining control, it is decreed: that the Cerro de Pasco Mining Company ordain, from this very day, that in every one of its shafts in present exploitation, be used automatic apparatus for unhooking the cable at its junction with the cage; that automatic seats be placed in the upper stations of the shafts, that the cages be provided with doors, which shall have to be closed when the vehicle be carrying occupants; that, to fill the place of an engine-driver the medical certificate be required, warranting the perfect state of health of the respective individual, as also a conduct–certificate, guaranteed by a trustworthy person and another testifying to the competence shown by the solicitant at some workshop, or to his having managed machinery at some other mine. Likewise it is decreed *that the engine–drivers shall never work over 8 hours running, and never put into motion a second winding-engine whilst another one is going, for two of these can only be allowed to work at the same* time, when handled by two different persons. As these measures tend to avoid the repetition of accidents, such as has happened yesterday; they must be adopted, generally, in all the mines where shafts are worked and in order that the preceding regulations be known to all miners, the Secretary shall pass a circular for the purpose.—C. A. Portella.—Issued in my presence—Carlos S. del Risco.

THE REPORT OF MR. CARLOS A. PORTELLA, MINING DELEGATE OF CERRO DE PASCO

Mr. Portella, Mining Delegate, presented to the Director of Public Wokrs an extensive and minute report, dated March 12th 1909, showing the deficiencies in the conduct of the mining work of the North-American Company, which gave rise to a large number of accidents. This document was the completest study which had as yet been made in Perú about so important an affair, and the criticisms which before had been published in the press of the province appeared pale at the side of its solid and scientific arguments. It showed moreover the serious omissions in the mining legislation of Perú, the error committed in allowing the high railway-tariffs, which caused the means of transport by rail to be a calamity instead of a benefit; the absence of whatever effort to advance the culture of the working class in the industrial companies and the cinical spirit displayed in the methods of exploitation in general.

Mr. Portella declared that the mines on a large and small scale were worked without heeding technical prescriptions; that the mining enterprises give no notice to the authorities of the people who are wounded in the operations of their industry; that the number of accidents is at least three or four times higher than that which becomes known to the public; that the work of perforation and the management of the explosives is performed without precaution of any kind; that preliminary tests are never made in the dangerous places of excavation; that explosives are accumulated within the interior of the mines, as though it were the same as depositing wood; that the dinamite is transported together with the detonators; that too many shots are fired at one time, without employing special matches; that the explosives are heated without taking precaution, these substances being handled as if they were like other inert ones; that the mines have only one outlet; that the metal is extracted, without filling up the open spaces as quickly as the extraction advances, leaving sometimes wells which have been worked, without putting in earth, with the object of diminishing the cost of the production.

The canalization and ventilation of the mines, the diverse systems of exploitation, the system to be employed at coal-mines, are also points regarded in the record we deal with. One result appears with the force of inexorable logic, from the report of the Delegate, namely, that the accidents in mines are not owing to unforeseeable and inevitable circumstances. On the contrary, they happen in consequence of the neglect and inhumanity of the managers of the business, and the sacrifice of the poor workmen is crowned by the contemptuous disobedience shown to the measures dictated by the Mining Delegation. The industrial sindicates come like an avalanche of conquest upon a primitive country. Our Government should remember that the great companies, full of presumption and without curb, only listen to the dictates of reason when they feel the weight of an energetic hand that imposes upon them inflexibly a pecuniary punishment.

THE CATASTROPHES IN THE COAL-MINES OF GOLLARISQUISGA

The first explosion occurred on January 23 d 1910 at the place called "Pique Chico", level G., the dead and wounded being numerous, as we have already said.

In consequence of this accident, the labours in this place were suspended until 9 th August of the same year, on which date they were resumed. On the following day; August 10 th, came the second terrible explosion, at 5 minutos to 5 p. m.

This was pay-day; the people were preparing to receive their salaries. Two watches of labourers were in the mine, under command of the foreman Carlos Valle, who had taken charge of the men of his colleague of level F., foreman Tur, who was absent. Before the two watches, composed of 310 men, left the mine, a dinamite shot was fired, causing the explosion.

The special correspondent of "La Prensa", a Lima daily, sent an ample account to his paper, from which we take many details which may as well precede the official report of Messrs. Habich and Bravo. Here goes an extract of his correspondence:

"Officially, the death of 67 persons has been announced on this occasion. Notwithstanding, if we calculate that 310 labourers were in the mine, of whom 67 were killed, 50 or 60 rescued, and 40 wounded, there would still remain 143, whose fate is ignored.

The special correspondent witnessed the burial of 72 corpses, but came to know that other victims were buried clandestinely and that some human remnants were covered with earth when the arrival of the Prefect and the rest of authorities was announced.

"The dinamite-shots", continues the correspondence, "must be made after the gangs have left and not while they remain in the mine, as happened on the 10 th. Against rule, Hercules' dinamite is used, the same being deposited, also against rule, in considerable quantities within the interior of the mines, in the so-called stores. Security lamps were not used; 30 shots at a time were allowed to explode, of which each one was lighted by seven cartridges; it was usual to light 50 shots of this kind at 11 in the morning and 150 or 200 at 5 p. m. The foremen were not present during these operations, and for this reason the Indians, when there was no clay at hand, used coal-dust, which is highly inflammable. There is hardly any vigilance exercised over the work by the superior employées.

An Italian foreman had issued with his gang before the explosion, saying that it was a barbarous proceeding to light 30 shots of dinamite with the people inside. Foreman Carlos Valle fell a victim to his servile devotion to the Company.

The absence of rescuing material was complete, not even a litter was to be found. Three attempts to save the victims were frustrated, because the people who went near the mine were choked. For such cases a kind of masks are provided, which hold air for two hours, and help to enter places which are invaded by poisonous gases, but no such contrivance had ever reached Gollarisquisga. It being impossible to descend into the mine without those masks, the possibility of rescue was almost excluded by this culpable omission and several of the first, intrepid rescuers died suffocated. An hour of struggle passed before any wounded were extracted from the place. In those humanitarian efforts distinguished themselves the superintendent of the mine, Frank Rally (or Fall), some medical men, labourers etc. More than 8 hours afterwards, at 1 ½ ó clock in the morning, arrived a train from Cerro de Pasco, bringing help, which was then almost superfluous.

The local chief of the police only seemed to have received the charge, from the Company, to custody the money which had been brought down for the payment, and to tell the people that the accident was nothing. The labour contractor (*enganchador*) R. Arístides Castro, spoke in quechua to the poor workmen, advising them not to be afraid and go to work, and that 5 cents (of a dollar) more would be paid to them, and that furthermore, the usual discount of 5 cents daily, for the oil which they burnt, would be retired.

THE COMPANY'S CONTEMPT FOR THE WORKMEN

(*Taken from the correspondence of the special envoy of "La Prensa" and the official report of Mssrs. Habich and Bravo.*)

The dead bodies were thrown into the stables, from which place they were removed by order of the prefect, as soon as this gentleman became aware of the fact through the protests of the relatives and comrades of the deceased.

The Company ordered immediately a quantity of oblong chests to be made, into which were collected the dispersed remnants of human bodies which were found in the vicinity of the site of the explosion. Amongst the perished was a father who embraced his son of 15 years old. The wakes over the horribly mutilated corpses were celebrated at the habitations of the workmen, these being narrow rooms of 2 ½ yards in depth by 2 in width. There the dead remained for 48 hours, exhaling intolerable odours. Not a single representative of the Company was present at the burial of the imfortunate victims; the cold heart of the capitalists could not be moved even by that spectacle of grief and desolation to give a sign of fellow-feeling for the poor Indian slave.

The dead and wounded were brought out of the place of the disaster on the shoulders of their surviving companions, in default of any instrument of succour. Many lives were lost simply because of the want of necessary elements. The North-Americans applied aseptic acid dissolved in water and liquid ammonium as a remedy for the suffocated. One of the so-called physicians of the Company diagnosticated a case of suffocation as an attack of alcoholism, for which reason the Official Commission advises Government not to accede to the petition of reconsideration, presented by the Company, against the decree which ordains, that the doctors employed in the hospitals of mining companies must be professionally qualified under the Peruvian laws.

The so-called hospital of Gollarisquisga is barely a place where the victims of some accident can be provisionally attended, and the requirements of the present case made it necessary that the Prefect should take all the wounded with him by train to Cerro de Pasco.

Can a greater contempt towards mankind be imagined, than this utter neglect in which the millionaire company of Cerro de Pasco had kept its workmen?

THE INDEMNIZATIONS

The Company paid all the expenses of the funeral, it being arranged that the accounts it owed to the victims should be paid immediately, to their nearest kindred and the obligations in its own favour relating to those that perished, be definitely cancelled.

On the other hand, the Prefect of Junin delivered to each family £ 1, as a present from Government.

Our readers will be aware that the catastrophe in question happened before the promulgation of the law of 20 th January 1911, so that the claims for indemnization were beholden to the dispositions contained in art. 12 of the by-law about contracts for services in the mining industry (*) except in those cases in which the labourers had made special arrangements with the contracting agents (enganchadores). The workmen who had come from the province of Jauja, to whom belonged the great majority of the victims, had agreed with the enganchador Castro to accept the sum of £. 20 as an indemnization in case of accident. It was arranged between the Company and the Official Commission that this money should be paid to the relatives at Jauja in the presence of the mining delegate, so as to make sure of the right

---

(*) *See note D.*

delivery. However the Company evaded this agreement, returning the families of the deceased to Jauja, by a train it dispatched without waiting for the mining delegate, who was to arrive from Cerro de Pasco. It is worth while to mention that those people went in cage cars, destined for the conduction of cattle.

The healing of the wounded, who were well attended at the Cerro de Pasco hospital, under the care of the Prefect, was, of course, paid by the Company. The patients received also a gift of £. 1 from Government, and the Company acknowledged the obligation to pay them their daily wages in full until the date of their total restablishment and to grant them an indemnization, the amount of which was to be accorded with the mining delegate, in those cases in which a full or partial inhabilitation for work should have supervened.

OTHER DETAILS FROM THE OFFICIAL REPORT: THE MANAGEMENT OF THE WORK.

The perforations are charged with one or two cartridges (weighing half an English pound each) of carbonite, this being an explosive which is allowed for mining uses in the United States. In the principal galleries, chests with clay are provided, for the purpose of forcing the shots, but it happens that the Indians, not being well watched, use coal-dust, instead, which is highly inflammable.

The foremen note down in a special book, the state of ventilation and gases in the mines, but the Commission can not affirm that a proper inspection of the mines takes place before each gang of men enters to work.

On the whole, the system of forcing the shots employed at Cerro de Pasco is that called in North-America "shooting off the solid", which ought to be prohibited on account of the danger it envolves.

The supply of water is scant in the mine. The principal galleries are lighted by electricity. In the by-works the men wear lamps fastened to their caps.

The coal of Gollarisquisga is rich in gases, which evaporate at a relatively low temperature, and much inclined to crumble into powder, which easily disperses, owing to the dryness of the mines.

It seems that until now, the grisu has not appeared in this mine, although its absence can not be proved, as the necessary instruments to test the air with regard to the grisu it might contain, can neither be supplied from Lima, nor by the Company.

The lamps ought to be nourished with alcohol or bencine, and not with oil, as is actually the case.

The explosion was probably caused by the fact that the shafts had not been sufficiently wetted.

The Commission regards as a principle cause of this explosion and the anterior ones. (viz. that of January and another two of which no notice was given to the Mining Delegation and of which resulted 5 or 7 wounded) the system of "shooting off the solid".

The Commission finds that neglects and technical defects in the work have contributed to produce the catastrophe; that a want of professional competence and a forgetfulness of the elementary rules of prudence in the exploitation of so notoriously dangerous a material as coal has become evident.

With the exception of the use of safety-powder, the Mining Company has obeyed none of the prescriptions contained in the supreme decree of 28th January 1910 (*); not having provided a single means of rescue, nor a gang of men dedicated to that purpose; there were not even litters to carry away the wounded; everything of the kind had to be brought from Cerro de Pasco, with the consequent delay.

Neither did the Company follow any of the measures dictated by the Mining Delegation after the similar accident of 23d January; and all this shows the little, or no respect which the Company has for the prescriptions of the legitimate authorities, principally when they demand expense for their execution.

The power of the explosion may best be appreciated by knowing the damages it caused, which are specialized in one part of the record.

THE MEASURES WHICH OUGHT TO BE ADOPTED IN ORDER TO AVOID FUTURE ACCIDENTS

The technical capacity of the directors of the work in the mines and the obligatory and regular inspection of the work by government officials must be insisted upon.

The revalidation, subject to severe rules, of the foreign engineer certificates (*which often are conceded with reckless prodigality, when they are issued for the exercise of the profession outside the country that gives the diplomas*) is necessary, as an indispensable security of real aptitude.

One observes certain unequivocal signs of rebellion on the part of the Company, continues saying the report, for all the measures recommended are either imperfectly applied, or not at all, as soon as they are considered to be expensive or troublesome, and owing to this circumstance, a constant and energetic

---

(*) See note E.

supervision is absolutely necessary to ensure the exact observance of rules.

The possible success of reforms would be very small, if an extreme vigilance were not established by the administration of the mine and care were not taken to advert the entire working body of the dangers to which it is exposed and of the means it must employ to avoid them; the only way to obtain this being a series of frequent explanations to the superior employées.

The system of "shooting off the solid" must be abolished immediately and for ever in the mine of Gollarisquisga and replaced by that of "undercutting" or "shearing".

The Commission is of opinion that a term of three months at the most, will suffice for the acquisition of the respective machinery in a number large enough to meet the exigencies of the present exploitation.

For the moment the work in the level G. will have to be stopped.

Another urgent measure is an increase of the water-supply and the careful removal of the accumulated coal-dust, which we have found in the levels I and G.

Before the shots are fired, the foremen must make an inspection in the shafts, to see that they are duly moistened.

It must also be a rule, that no shots may be fired before all the gangs have issued from the shaft.

The record adds several technical prescriptions, referring to the shots and the security lamps, which we will not mention in detail so as not to make this review any longer, it being our aim only to arouse the attention of those who are called to make a formal investigation of the methods employed by the Cerro de Pasco Mining Co.

At least two gangs of rescuers ought to be ready always, nor should be wanting, as happens at present, a due provision of the indispensable material of assistance, which at the time of the last catastrophe arrived 4 hours too late, and even then, incomplete, from Cerro de Pasco.

Furthermore, the Company must be obliged to effect a total reparation and cleansing of the Gollarisquisga hospital. In this establishment, exist now only 3 beds, and the operation table there may serve as an eloquent example of the reigning neglect.

Considering the utter disregard shown by the Company towards the orders of the respective authorities, energetic proceedings will have to be resorted to for the purpose of enforcing obedience to rules, and a scale of fines ought to be established, beginning with £. 1000 minimun, to punish the abuses, it being practicable also in cases of serious faults or frequent relapses, to suspend the work for some length of time.

The Mining Delegation remitted a copy of most of the

above-mentioned prescriptions, which were sure to be officially sanctioned, to the Mining Company, so as to prevent the latter's alleging ignorance of the same.

The accident of 10th August only damaged the work of preparation and not that of extraction at the Gollarisquisga mine, so that the latter could be continued without difficulty.

At the end, the report names the acts of heroism executed during the work of rescue, by the superintendent Francisco Fall (or Frank Rally), the engineer Aurelio Ruiz Huidobro, the foreman of level E., Luis Flores, and the police sargeants of Cerro de Pasco, Acosta and Ballesteros. The authorities and the physicians Portella and Anchorena, also lent good services in their own sphere of action.

AT CONGRESS

A deputy at Congress, Mr. Carlos Lora y Quiñones, addressed on 23d August 1910 an official letter to the Minister of Public Works, in which he refers to a denouncement made in the Lima dailies, saying that the Company had recommenced work in the coalmine of Gollarisquisga, immediately after the official investigating commission had left; of course, without effecting any of the required reforms and acting simply in accordance with its habit of disregarding government orders.

Dr. Joaquín Capelo said in the Senate, on 24th October of the same year, that the decree issued by Government on 26th August, after hearing the report of the Official Commission, declared that the pending accounts of the victims of the accident should be cancelled by the Company and that, according to a report presented by the Asociacion Pro-Indígena, which was published in the Lima press and not contradicted by any one, it was known that a quantity of such accounts had not been cancelled, and that, instead, the families of the victims of the catastrophe, suffered persecutions in Jauja to make them pay what was owed by those who lost with their lives whatever they had to lose.

In the same session the above-named senator presented a law-project, tending to protect the Indians against the despotism of the great industrials. The document was passed over to a parliamentary commission.

POSTERIOR ACCIDENTS

On September 23d the Lima newspapers announced the occurrence of two new accidents at Gollarisquisga, which caused 8 victims.

On 2d October of the same year were killed 4 labourers by a crash in a mine. The pressure of the roof broke the supports between the levels C and D, not leaving the men time to escape.

"El Minero Ilustrado" of that date gives the news that the

superintendent Frank Fall or Rally had resigned his post, on account, it seems, of the too frequent accidents which happened in the mines of Gollarisquisga.

Juan de la C. Enriquez, timberman of the said mine, appealed on 13th February 1911 to the Asociación Pro-Indígena, in consequence of not having been regarded, after an accident he suffered, neither with assistance at the hospital, nor with payment of his wages, nor having found help in his claims against the Company at the Mining Delegation, whose duty it is, according to the Mining Code, to attend to such affairs.

With this case begins the period in which the victims of accidents had a right to place themselves under the protection of the law of 20th January 1911, which has also been, as we shall see, a meaningless document for the Company.

"El Minero Ilustrado" of 28th April 1911 says that the tax of £. 5 for a man killed is the only one that has ruled, rules, and will rule to pay for any misfortune that happens at the mines of the Cerro de Pasco Co., in the face of any law that may be dictated to the contrary. In the same number reference is made to three accidents occurred during the week:

1 Max W. Jorgensen, of German nationality, was killed by the lift, in the shaft "Noruega".

2 Nicanor Mandujano, at Gollarisquisga, killed, because the descending car was thrown against a post.

3 Andrés Sarmiento, 12 years old, was buried under the ruins of a part of the mine "San Anselmo", which collapsed.

This shaft was worked for Mr. Joseph Flemming, manager of the Company.

The "Minero Ilustrado" of 5th July says that on the Saturday before, Felipe Salcedo became the victim of a hitch in the machinery of the cage of the central shaft, and died after two days in the Company's hospital. In such cases the Company declares that it has no responsibility in the accident in order to refuse payment of indemnization, and no one will prove the contrary, for the persons who are called for witnesses are the Company's own employées, who would lose their post if they did not render testimony in accordance with the interests of their employers.

Salcedo left in misery a widow and 4 children.

"*The managers of the business, who formerly granted sometimes the poor sum of £. 5, under condition of receiving a signed document in which the relatives of the victim declared that the Company had no responsibility whatever in the accident, deny to-day with utmost hardness even this small succour* (because the new law for labour accidents declares null and void the importance of such documents), *thus reducing to the last destitution the families of the men who give their lives for their master's profit.*"

With these words ends the paragraph in the "Minero Ilustrado."

As several members of the Asociación Pro-Indígena had published articles in the Lima press about the case of Salcedo, the same as they did before regarding the example of Juan de la C. Enriquez, the Mining Co. deemed it convenient to publish on its part a reply to those observations in the newspapers, signed by its representative J. M. Schultheiss, which resulted to be a total failure, if considered as a refutation of the denouncements made. The legal declaration drawn up at the Mining Delegation of Cerro de Pasco, after Salcedo's misfortune, which Mr. Schultheiss encloses, in his letter to the press, states that the reason of the accident was: the breaking of the copper ledge which keeps in position the automatic unhooking apparatus of the cable, which caused the cage to fall and gives injunctions for the strict vigilance and daily cleansing of the ropes and security contrivances, as also the frequent inspection of the bars and bolts of the automatic unhooking apparatus used in the shafts; the renewal of these latter every two months, taking especial care to observe their state of brittleness, to avoid ruptures, etc. Consequently, at the proper time, these necessary rules of precaution had not been observed.

The indemnization paid to Salcedo's family, which is mentioned in the letter, was granted after the publication of the denouncements.

On 6th and 8th July 1911 perished in two succeeding accidents at Gollarisquisga, the workmen Liberato Melgarejo and Leopoldo Naupari, whose widows were seen for many days at the Company's lawyer's office, pleading to obtain the humble indemnization that the managers might chose to give them.

On 20th September 1911 were killed by suffocation in the central shaft of Cerro de Pasco, three workmen, named Roberto Fraser, a foreigner, Faustino Mejía and Francisco Caro, natives. As the Company took advantage of the victim's families not knowing the import of the law of 20th January 1911, for the purpose of paying no indemnization, the Asociación Pro-Indígena explained to the relatives of the perished labourers the benefits of that law, indicating to them the sum they had a legal right to claim, according to the time of service and value of the wages.

Faustino Mejía has a brother, disabled for work because he broke one of his feet, on 17th April 1910, in the service of the Company, without ever having received an indemnization for that accident.

October 27th 1911, the workmen Silvino M. Salazar and Manuel Hidalgo were buried under a huge mass of loose mineral. It seems that for this accident, and similar ones which occurred before, was responsible Mr. Olson, chief of a gang, who obliged his people with threats to enter into perilous places without taking the least precaution to avoid the exposal of their lives.

The Company alleged that those two victims had left no relatives, intending to elude, as ever, any kind of obligation.

The Asociación Pro-Indígena undertook to find out, whether the deceased had no kindred in Huamalíes and Jauja, the places they came from, and sent a circular to its provincial delegates, calling upon them to dissuade the Indians from entering into contracts with a Company which showed itself so ungrateful to the services of its workmen.

2d November 1911 a fire broke out in the exploitation—field N. 101 at Cerro de Pasco. Although the Mining Delegate, Portella, and the Prefect, Puente y Olavegoya, tried to hush up the importance of this accident in the telegrams they sent to Lima, the correspondent of "La Prensa" communicated to his paper on the same date, 4th November, as follows: "Last night 7 labourers were extracted, almost dead, with suffocation, and to-day another 7 have been brought out in a deplorable state. People say that in the interior of the gallery are more than 50 men, in danger of suffocation. The captain of the shaft, Olson, obeying orders of the Company, forces the miners to work in the conflagrated region, with no regard to the security of their lives."

A further telegram from the same correspondent appears on November 5th: "The fire took larger proportions, a spontaneous combustion having set in at the central shaft; the men were forced to penetrate into the site of danger, with the object of quenching the same; 16 miners returned with symptoms of suffocation, and they are treated, together with other invalids, at the North-American hospital."

"All the respective authorities were on the spot, dictating measures to obtain the prompt extinction of the fire. Luckily, on this occasion, no deaths are to be lamented."

El "Minero Ilustrado" of 13th December 1911 tells of an earthslip in the mining works of the zone "Peña Blanca", at Cerro de Pasco, which could have been foreseen for a long time and had been preceded already by several smaller accidents. The Company proposed to hush up this event, and it was only owing to the denouncement made by the widow of the workman Aniceto Basualdo, that the authorities presented themselves to practice an ocular inspection of the spot.

The unfortunate widow of Basualdo had appealed, with a newborn infant in her arms, at the lawyer's office of the Company, on behalf of her husband, but failed to move with her entreaties the heart of the legal adviser, who was already too much accustomed to such spectacles. Basualdo, a man of 37 years of age, was still lying at the time, under the ruins of the earthslip.

A telegram of 26th March 1912 from Cerro de Pasco, says: "Last night, the workman N. Eloy was unjustly taken prisoner by the Commissioner of the foundry, Miguel Malpartida, and taken to the police office, where in the morning he was found dead. It is feared that he will be buried without undergoing dissection, or that, as in the case of the labourer Mansilla, the doctor's certificate will be rejected as false, all for the purpose of leaving unpunished a crime. The contents of this telegram are confirmed by a second one of 27th March.

12th April 1912 the crash of a mineral bridge in the interior of the mine "Excelsior" at Cerro de Pasco, occasioned the instantaneous death of the contractor Alberto Quispe, and serious wounds to the labourers Domingo Alfaro, Ricardo Flores, Nicolás Espinoza and Canuto Raymundo, who were taken to the Company's hospital.

Quispe was a contractor of perforating work in the mine San Anselmo; 25 years old; he met with his doon on the first morning that he worked there in a new capacity, and the cause of his death was attributable to the mean economy of the Company, which omitted to effect some works of support in the place where the accident occurred, and moreover obliged Quispe to fire several shots in so dangerous a region.

The family of the deceased obtained for all indemnization £. 2 ½ and an ill-made coffin.

In the afternoon of 15th April 1912, perished in the already frequently mentioned central shaft, young Manuel R. Artete, a man much esteemed for his moral qualities and an old employée of the Company, a carpenter, who was likewise obliged to execute some work under insufficient conditions of security, so that, whilst trying to extricate an implement, he lost his balance and fell into the bottom of the shaft, remaining lifeless, and his body converted into a shapeless heap of bones. His comrades gave an honourable burial to his remains, but it is left to be seen as yet, what may be the indemnization which the Company will grant.

6th March 1912, Cirilo Sosa, aged 25 years, had his right hand destroyed by an accident, whilst working at a machine in the foundry, after having served there for 6 years and a half, receiving lately a salary of 1 dollar 50 cents. He was more than three months at the hospital of Cerro de Pasco, badly attended, as regards medical assistance and diet. Discharged at last from this establishment, he presented himself to the superintendent of the Company, Mr. Spilburg, demanding the wages due for the last month which he worked and the half wages to which he had a right during his illness, and asking besides to be awarded the pension for life, which the law of 20th January 1912 fixes for cases like his own. Mr. Spilburg assented only to the first of the above claims, waving the second one and as to the third, he offered to Sosa as a final indemnization the sum of £. 10 gold, it being necessary for the reader to know, that the amount payable to him under the reigning law would be £. 108. Not even would Mr. Spilburg consent to give the man a certificate, mentioning the time he worked at the foundry, and the circumstance of the accident which invalidated him for all his life.

Sosa says that Mr. Spilburg has got a reputation for his inhuman treatment of the labourers and that he persisted in his negative to give a certificate, although recommendatory letters from the Manager of the Company and the Prefect of Junin were presented to him.

The disabled man sustained his parents by his work, who are to-day threatened by misery, the same as himself.

27th July 1912 the mine "San Anselmo" at Cerro de Pasco collapsed, for want of measures of security and provision taken by the superintendents of the work. Two workmen were killed and several wounded by this accident, the consternation being great at Cerro de Pasco on account of these news.

On 19th and 22d of August occurred two accidents, at level E of the mines of Gollarisquisga. The victims were Predicación Ferreros, from the village Muqui of the province of Jauja, and N. Huari, of the village Tusi, of the province of Cerro de Pasco, both married, leaving a widow and small children. They were buried in an open field, which the Company has dedicated now to the object of interring the bodies of its victims and the surviving kin received no indemnization.

Ferreros was an *enganchado* (contracted workman) and was obliged to work near a large block of coal, which, coming down violently, caused his instantaneous death.

The other man, Huari, was posted on the line of the elevator at level E., without receiving instructions how to avoid the car which was running there and surely enough caught him in its rapid career, killing him on the spot. The accident was discovered by the commissioner, who noticed the marks of blood on the car. Upon his indication, the employées penetrated into the interior of the mine, finding Huari still with the last signs of life.

A TYPICAL DOCUMENT

We give the following example of one of those documents, which the Company uses to formulate in order to elude whatever compromise on account of the accidents which happen to its employées:

"This document is to state the following facts:"

"That in the month of May last, *by a casual accident* in the Smelter, *I resulted hurt with a burn in the eye.*"

"That the Cerro de Pasco Mining Company, owner of the said smelter in whose service I worked; took me to the Cerro de Pasco Hospital to be healed and that I, by my own free will, left that hospital, without the consent of the medical attendant, Dr. W. C. Macdonald."

"That according to the certificate given by Dr. E. Campodónico (at Lima) *my cure was finished on 20th July last.*"

"That the Company in question has agreed to pay me, *without being obliged to do so,* as a full indemnization, my wages for 54 days, during which I could not work, by reason of my illness, reckoned at 4 soles a. day. (1)

"That I receive *to my entire satisfaction* the sum of two hundred and sixteen soles silver ($. 216), as the amount of those 54 working days."

"That I renounce the claim to any other indemnization and also the liberty to initiate any legal action which I might raise against the Cerro de Pasco Mining Company on account of the accident or my cure at Lima."

"I sign this document in the presence of witnesses."

"La Fundición, 8th November 1906."

(signed:) "*Nicolás Díaz.*"

We have written in italics some of the paragraphs of this notable document, in order to emphathize the monstruosities it contains.

In the first place, the reader must be adverted that the burn in the eye means the loss of the right eye for the sufferer, Nicolás Díaz.

The document does not express this, when it says that the cure was complete on 20th July, the date of Dr. Campodónico's certificate.

In the second place, the Company affirms that it was not obliged to grant an indemnization for this accident, it being the fact that it had the duty to do so, even under de insufficient law which ruled before the present one of 20th January 1912, in case the misfortune was not due only to a punishable neglect on the part of the victim. The Company would be unable to prove the responsibility of Díaz on this occasion, and moreover, it is worth while to mention that shortly after the event were suddenly discharged from their positions the superintendent, John I. Case, the general engineer, Mr. Adams and the engineer of the workshop, Mr. Thomas.

Under such circunstances, it was impossible that Díaz should receive. *to his entire satisfaction*, the amount of the half-wages due to him for the time of his sickness, as an only indemnization for an accident which reduced the work he could do to half its former value, as we shall see further on. After Díaz was healed in Lima, the Company, knowing his aptitude, offered him a place worth 3 dollars 25 cents daily wages, at the smelter, but finding that the want of an eye incapacitated him for certain kinds of work, it removed him to another workshop, where he only earned 2 dollars, this being the reason why Díaz retired from the Company, having a large family to support.

---

(1) this means half wages, for the smelter in question earmed 8 soles, that is 4 dollars, a day.

Díaz would not continue at the Cerro de Pasco Hospital, on account of its excessively bad conditions, as he openly told the Company in a paper which was signed by 14 persons who knew the establishment from their own experience.

The document in which Díaz renounces all claims beyond the 108 dollars for the daily half wages payable during his illness, was signed, not because the man concerned thought its stipulations equitable, but because, without his signing it, the Company would not have paid him a single cent in the miserable situation to which he was then reduced.

THE CERRO DE PASCO HOSPITAL

Another very interesting document is the first demand of indemnization for a labour accident put in by Julio Coltellini at the Mining Delegation against the Cerro de Pasco Mining Co., which gives besides an idea of the kind of assistance offered to the patients at the hospital sustained by the obligatory monthly contributions of the Company's employees and workmen:

"To the Mining Delegate:

I, Julio Coltellini, residing at Dos de Mayo Street, N. 12, appear before you, saying: that on 17th July last, at 3 ó clock in the afternoon, more or less, I became the victim of an accident in the shaft "Diamante" of the Cerro de Pasco Mining Company, where I worked as timberman.

I was working in the stope N. 48 of level 200, when a loosening of the earth, or small slide, occurred, and a stone fell on my brain, causing me the complete loss of my left eye. And this is not even the most serious part of the case, for, in consequence of the blow I suffered, I have become subject to cerebral attacks, so that I might say, I am disabled for work.

The Cerro de Pasco Mining Company, took me to the hospital after the accident, where no care was taken either to attend nor to cure me; and seeing the negligence revealed there, I resolved to repair to Lima, for surely, in the contrary case, I should have died. So wonderful and surprising was the indolence of the Company, that my wound was not even washed, and the physician in Lima, Dr. Juvenal Denegri, was greatly astonished to find it mixed with matters provening from the earth-slide and in dirty condition altogether.

Hereby are added the two certificates given by Dr. Juvenal Denegri, which testify to the seriousness of the wound.

This earth-slide may be considered as one of the results of the disastrous ill-management of the Cerro de Pasco Mining Company's works, this enterprise being anxious only to extract, metal, without paying any heed to the dangers incurred by its workmen.

Thus, the Conpany orders its men to work at excavations

which are not filled up, and where it is almost inevitable that accidents should occur, like the one that happened to me. In this sense, the responsibility of this accident and that of all the others which occur, is imputable to the Company, for these events are produced, not by an unavoidable fatality, but through sheer contempt for human life. Doubtlessly, the Cerro de Pasco Mining Co. has not fulfilled either the prescript contained in art. 8 of the Ordinance of Mining Police, for it hides in darkness all the accidents which happen in its mines, as long as they do not cause the death of the workmen, just as if the invalidation of a labourer for all his life were not worse than death.

As I have contracted a hurt which disables me for normal work, in a permanent manner, a hurt acquired in the act of working and through the same, I can appeal to the dispositions contained in art. 12 of the Ordinance for Labour Contracts in the Mining Industry; therefore:

I ask of you that you will issue an order to the Cerro de Pasco Mining Company, obliging it to pay me a pension equal to half of the salary I earned, calculated for a term of three years, my salary having been 3 dollars a day.

Moreover I add that the enclosed certificates be returned to me and a copy of them left in the warrants.

Cerro de Pasco, October 14th 1908."

Julio Coltellini."

"Medical Certificates:

HOSPITAL "VICTOR MANUEL"

The undersigned physician certifies: that Mr. Julio Coltellini, miner of Cerro de Pasco, entered this hospital, on 23d of this month, with a fracture of the scull and depression of the same, and an extensive bruise in the left front bone region, *completely infected*, and in such a state that it puts his life into serious danger.—Lima, July 26th 1908.—Dr. Juvenal Denegri.

A seal.

The undersigned physician certifies that Mr. Julio Coltellini has been treated, at this hospital, from July 23d up to this day, for a wound from a blow in the left front bone region, with depression of the scull and a detachment of the retina, consequent upon this traumatism.—Lima, 6th October 1908.- Dr. Juvenal Denegri."

....

Eugenio Camarena, from the town of Jauja, 33 years old, had been working for 5 years at the coal-mines of Vinchuscancha. Having fallen into the water, by accident, he got sick of an inflammation of the lungs and died at the Cerro de Pasco Hospital. The Company had offered to the widow a sum of money in exchange of the life of her husband, but when she went to the hospital to obtain the death-certificate, she was summarily rejected and thrown out of the establishment. At last the superintendent, Mr. Stone, gave her 6 dollars to pay the funeral expenses. This was in February 1909.

Fidel Villayzán, from Junin, already mentioned elsewhere, who had fallen to the ground from the height of one of the chimneys, which were at that time being constructed at Smelter, and resulted with a wound in his head and a luxation of the right leg, was taken to the Cerro de Pasco Hospital and placed in a corner, without a bed, and no assistance given to him, until his relatives saw the necessity of taking him away and having him cured at their own expense.

When Nicolás Díaz was at the Hospital, a plate of dried peas and potatoes was brought to him in the morning, and as he did not feel like eating this meal, the same plate was brought to him again in the evening, for dinner, warmed up, and he was told, that no other diet was prepared for any of the patients.

June 2d 1909 a young workman, Vicente Cerrón, was hurt by an earth-slide in the mine Diamante, and as he refused to go to the Hospital, fearing that his foot would be amputated, the Company denied him the half wages wich are due to the men who have suffered accidents of this kind.

The Company, adding despotism to negligence, punishes the people, as we see, for not going to its Hospital. The physieian of the establishment, Macdonald, named by Díaz, is the one that continues there to-day, as far as we know.

THE STRIKES

Strikes are rare in the mining and agricultural districts of Perú, as may be inagined, when considering the character of the workmen, wo are so submissive and accustoned to all kinds of privations.

In September 1908 a terrible explosion occurred at the mine "Peña Blanca" of Cerro de Pasco, caused, firstly, by the dilation of the masses of mineral through the chemical reaction of the sulphur which exists in the shaft, and secondly, by the bad conduction of the work, the mineral being extracted in considerable quantities, leaving enormous cavities, which are places of danger and death to the workmen; the greatest majority of those who form the terrible death-roll of the Cerro de Pasco Company's mines, having perished in such places.

Terrified by that catastrophe, the workmen contracted in the district of Chongos, in the province of Huancayo, retired altogether from Cerro de Pasco, and returned to their home, at the risk of facing the difficulties which the contracting agent there, Ignacio Matos, would raise against them. The Company wanted to oblige them to work again in the same mine, notwithstanding its being in imminent danger of a new collapse, and, by means of compulsion, it denied to them the acknowledgment of their having worked already for a fortnight on account of their contract with the said Mr. Matos. Amongst the labourers who left Cerro de Pasco, appear the names of Evaristo Perez, Ildefonso Patilla, Benito Yanrivilca, Santiago García, José Vilcapoma, Francisco Naña, Mateo Chávez, Evaristo de la Cruz, Buenaventura Raya, and Pedro Vilcapoma.

In June 1909, the firemen of the Cerro de Pasco Railway Company declared a strike, asking that the hours of work be reduced to nine a day, that their salary be raised to 15 £. a month and personal merits be taken into consideration when promotions were made. These demands were presented verbally, without any acts of violence being resorted to nor any subversive demonstrations being made.

The "Eco de Junin" of 26th June of that year, affirms that the Company promised revenge to the leader of the strikers, Mr. Washington Oviedo, and after having this man taken to prison twice, with the authorization of the Prefect, Mr. Argote, and not being able to attribute to him any culpability, it contrived to involve him in a scandal at its offices, which ended by his being accused of insubordination to the police, this pretext being sufficient to put him definitely into jail, notwithstanding the protests that came from eye-witnesses of the scene and from members of the police itself. The omnipotent Company could not allow the pretension of being incommodated by strikes and the political authority was hipnotized completely enough with its suggestions, to connive in the plan of punishing Oviedo, submitting him to a court-martial, which lends itself easier to summary justice than the common law-tribunals. It was said at the same time, that the Company deported from Cerro de Pasco, in one of its trains, other five strikers, thus incurring in a perfectly illegal proceeding, as can well be understood.

The principal culprits of these intrigues seem to have been the Company's employée Mr. Mc. Geary and the lawyer Chiriboga.

In general, it must be adverted, that the North-American employées behave to their subordinates according to the category these belong to, paying certain considerations to the skilled artizans, and throwing all the weight of their contempt on the unlucky, ignorant journeymen, who form the great mass of their dependents.

Also in 1909, the workmen of the Cerro de Pasco Company twice declared a strike, on account of the hostile treatment observed towards the most ancient servants of the enterprise, whose wages were reduced without any motive. None of the compromises accepted in order to put an end to the strike were kept by the representatives of the Company.

Finally it was agreed that the labourers should receive 1 dollar a day and 25 cents for extra hours. However, it must not be believed that such a tariff was made general at Cerro de Pasco.

In April 1912 the workmen of the Company declared a

strike because they were requested to pay the carbure which is daily consumed in their lamps, this being an affair which we already mentioned whilst speaking of the arrangements celebrated after the second catastrophe at Gollarisquisga, on 10th August 1911.

As at that period (April 1912) a formidable strike convulsed the agricultural district of Chicama, in the department of La Libertad, the Company was afraid that a similar movement might invade its own precincts, and acceded immediately to the petition of the workmen, so that the labours were stopped only one day.

LATEST NEWS FROM GOLLARISQUISGA AND SMELTER.

At present, in 1912, the Company has taken perhaps some precautions at Gollarisquisga, in order to avoid a repetition of that horrible series of catastrophes we have mentioned; certainly on behalf of its own interest and not on that of humanity. The work at the coal mine is carried on, up to date, in the following manner: the guard for the day-work enters at 5 a. m., and has half an hour's rest, after 1 p. m, for the midday meal; it leaves the mine at 5 p. m. The night-guard enters at 7 p. m. and leaves at 5 a. m., working without interruption. The same guards' work alternately one week during the day and the following during the night, receiving a daily salary of 70 cents.

At Smelter the principal superintendent at present is Mr. Hamilton. There are only two Peruvians on the staff of upper employés, namely, Mr. Araujo, the second master of the traffiic department, and Mr. Benavides, the head-master of the carpenter's shop.

Mr. Spilburg, head-master of the camp, is reputed to have little tact in his general comportment, whereas the second master of the mechanic's shop, Mr. Roper, has won a good name amongst his subordinates.

Since the Cerro de Pasco Company began to work, the salaries have diminished rather than increased. Simple labourers get to-day half a dollar or 60 cents. Peruvians are paid lower salaries than foreigners in the same capacity, which is evidently wrong, for either the work is not well done, if they are less qualified, or they are treated unjustly, if they are equal to their competitors.

The men in the carpenter's shop earn 2 and 2 ½ dollars a day.

The electricians 1 ½ to 2 dollars.

At the machine shop 1, 1,25 and 1 ½ dollars.

The craneoperators, 2 dollars, when Peruvians and 5 dollars, when foreigners. These are exposed to all the hot vapours from the basins of smelted ore.

The fitters receive 90 cents, 1 dollar, 1,10 or 1,25; risking their lives near the heat of the furnace.

On the other hand the brakers, who have to go out at one or two 6'clock in the morning in snow and frost to turn the turn-table, receive 80, and 90 cents or from 1 to 1 dollar 10.

All this kind of work is so heavy and dangerous, at such an altitude moreover, that few people resist it for over three months at a stretch; the foreigners are given license to recover in Lima and the natives must discharge their system as best they can of the poisenous stuff deposited on their stomach and lungs.

In the power-house the men earn from 1 dollar 25 to 1, 50 or 1, 75. These are skilled artizans, who attend to the machines, the pumps, air compresses, oiling of the wheels in motion, etc.

In the boiler-house the firemen earned formerly 1 dollar 40; the coalmen from 75 to 90 cents. The guard was made up of 8 firemen and 8 coalmen. Since petroleum has been introduced as a combustible, the whole service, of attending to 32 furnaces, runs in charge of two men, who get 1 dollar 75 cents each.

The guard of stoppers in the blast furnace, who throw the ore and the coal into the furnaces, obtain from 75 cents to 1 dollar

The salary for the guard of triturators (chancadores), is 75 cents.

The men of the coke-implant, who form two guards, and burn two furnaces full of coal each, also have 75 cents a day. At the coalwash the daily wages ascend to the same, 75 cents.

The constructor's guard, employed in building the furnaces, receives a rate of 60 to 75 cents.

The convertor's guard is divided into two halves of which one earns 75 cents and the other 1 dollar.

The yard-guard has wages varying between 50 and 60 cents.

The houses for the employés, (some consisting of two rooms of the size of ten feet square, and others built of brick and concrete, consisting of two rooms 15 feet long by 14 feet broad) were let gratis at the beginning, but now pay a rent of half a dollar and one dollar a month, respectively. Altogether, the social organization is so deficient that the employés and artizans belonging to the decent class, can not have their families near them at Smelter.

Everything which big mining enterprises, like the Cerro de Pasco Company, would have to attend to gratuitiously in Europe and the United States, is here not attended to at all or subject to special contributions discounted from the daily wages of the workmen's and employées staff.

CONCLUSION.

In the chapter in which we speak of the accidents registered in the history of the Cerro de Pasco Mining Co., we have allowed the largest space to the catastrophe of Gollarisquisga of 10th August 1910, for the very important reason that on this occasion a very comprehensive official report was made, which as such has a particular value, and does certainly not tend to exaggerate the responsibilities that weigh on the managers of that enterprise.

The causes which produced the first catastrophe of Gollarisquisga, on Sunday 23d January 1910 were exactly the same as those which originated the second one, namely, the explosion occurred in consequence of the captains of the night-guard, Pedro Gava, having ordered 30 dinamite shots to be fired at a depth of 620 feet, where the air is so deficient that the men who work there issue half benumbed from the emanation of the gases.

The utter contempt which the Company feels for the interests and even the lives of its neighbours, is evinced at every opportunity, the same on a large as on a small scale, as in the instance when the municipality of Cerro de Pasco had to be appealed to for the purpose of enforcing that the pits of the mines, which are opened near frequented thoroughfares, be closed by fences to avoid accidents.

The Brazilian physician, Dr. Carlos Simoens da Silva, who visited the installations of the North-American enterprise in July 1910, after having paid the tribute of his admiration to the grandeur of the works, described as cruel the fact that no measures had been taken to mitigate the abrupt change which the miner has to undergo when emerging from the interior of the earth to the overground temperature. He says: "I could comprobate an infernal heat in the galleries, and a continual rising of sulphurous gases; in this temperature the men work for 12 hours, and then issue from the mine, meeting with a cold corresponding to a height of 4,330 metres over the level of the sea.

The average length of life of a miner in Perú is 5 years, for the human constitution does not resist for any further amount of time the system of work which one of the most colossal companies of the world has not been ashamed to adopt. For this end, the Indian is torn away, by cheat and fraud, from his rustic home, subjected to laws which only help to enslave him and persecuted by the soldiery when he tries to escape from his masters.

It seems to be true that, in order to calm the excitement of the survivors after the first catastrophe of Gollarisquisga, when the people crowded horrified around the outlet of the mine, a couple of brandy barrels was distributed amongst them, with the object that, during the ensuing state of drunkenness, the bodies of the victims might be extracted and quickly buried without being noticed.

With the bonds for the drinking shops a big business is

made by the dependents of the Cerro de Pasco Mining Co. Everybody knows that misery and alcoholism go together. The glass of brandy is the only compensation to be found for the mean wages and the intolerable climate, and the Company deals it out with both hands, of course, to its workmen, so as to keep them quiet under its extortions.

Here is an ample field of action for the members of anti-alcoholic leagues, the same as for special philanthropists and men of an upright conscience in general.

All the secrets hidden in the Smelter and the mines of Cerro de Pasco and Gollarisquisga will never be known. The engines will not tell of the human bones they have triturated, nor the glowing furnaces of the bodies they have consumed.

The tetrical horrors of those places may be put beside those of the rubber region of the Putumayo, which was named the Devil's Paradise. It has happened at the Smelter that the North-American employées, in a state of drunkenness, have got impatient when the Indian workers did not understand their orders, given in English, and pushed them by an impulsive movement into the flames of the furnace. The firemen perform their task in such a precarious position, that they are in continual and imminent danger of being caught by the trains that carry the coal to the mouth of the furnaces (*). If the "Minero Ilustrado" reckons in a leading article of last August at 1,500 the number of victims made by the North-American industry at Cerro de Pasco, it refers only to those killed and wounded through accidents, it being probable that this cipher might rise to 15,000 when taking into consideration the workmen who have died through sickness contracted in consequence of the criminal higienic neglects of the Company and the unnatural expenditure of physical energies demanded by the methods of exploitation in use.

We believe that the Head Management of the Cerro de Pasco Mining Company, resident in the United States, will take note of the present exposition of facts, which we make with all moderation and ample foundation, for if not, it would place itself into the same category as the house of Arana, at Iquitos, and we rest assured that the North-American public will insist, after knowing the truth, that the reputation of its country in the exterior be kept free from the slur which such proceedings as we have described, would reflect upon it.

As it is just as useful for our purpose to point out the good men, as the bad, who have actuated in the Cerro de Pasco Mining Co., we shall mention the name of Mr. I. W. Harris who, according to our references, possessed all the technical qualifications for the post he filled until the middle of the year 1908, when the Company began to replace the competent employées with inferior ones, the consequence being, that a fatal series of earth-slides set in at the mines of the place.

(*) *See note F.*

Doubtlessly, however, the competence of one single man is not a sufficient guarantee for the good conduct, in every detail, of so extensive a business as the Cerro de Pasco Mining Co.; which is distributed moreover. in various places, separated by long distances the one from the other. The Head-Management of this Company in the United States, is obliged not only to be very strict in the selection of the representatives and directors of their business in our country, but to organize a severe and constant control over the staff of employées who are in charge of the work at the mines and the smelter. If, as we hope, the said Board of Management be willing to attend to that duty, we offer our cooperation, as far as it is in our power to lend it, with knowledge gathered on the spot. We insist that the great nations will simply be the supporters of savagery in the world, whilst they continue protecting, as their citizens, those people who do not adhere in foreign countries to the principles of civilization which have been their rule at home.

In view of the intolerable state of affairs which prevails evidently at the dependencies, of the Cerro de Pasco Mining Company, the "Asociación Pro-Indígena" demanded that the same should be called before the tribunals of justice, in the following recourse which was presented to the Minister of Justice:

"Denounces the proceedings observed by the Cerro de Pasco Mining Co., towards the Indian labourers employed at its works and the indifference shown by the local judicial and political authorities.

Your Excellency:

I, Pedro S. Zulen. General Secretary of the Asociación Pro-Indígena, appear before Your Excellency, denouncing the atentatóry proceedings which the Cerro de Pasco Mining Co., a mining enterprise established in the province of Pasco, department of Junín, practises upon its Indian labourers, animated no doubt by a feeling of utter disrespect for the laws of the country and by the thorough impunity it enjoys in view of the culpable indifference of the public authorities.

More or less serious accidents occur with great frequency in the mines of the above-mentioned company, causing very often the death or inability for work of the labourers; these accidents being generally attributable to inhumanity, excessive economy, or lack of science in the conduct of the work and always to a disobedience of the officially prescribed rules. A mining delegate has his post at Cerro de Pasco, as well as a common judge, an official agent, a prefect, a sub-prefect, yet all these functionaries ever ignore or feign to ignore, the accidents which happen, just as if the respective territory did not belong to Perú, nor the sacrificed Indians were their fellow-citizens, but on the contrary, their duty required to protect every arbitrariness and crime.

For instance, on 20th July last, the labourers Marcial Rocano, and Estanislao Torres were buried under a mass of mineral in the mine "San Anselmo", which the said Company is working. The local weeklies "Los Andes" in its edition of July 23d and "El Minero Ilustrado" of the 24th, whilst denouncing the accident, complain of the indifference and silence of the authorities obliged to take note of such cases. The latter periodical says: "It is already four days that two of our fellow-men remain buried, in a mine without having received any help, without an attempt having been made to ascertain how they perished; and notwithstanding, not a word is spoken by the authorities, nor private persons, who seem to be afraid of the insolent and irresponsible power of a Company enriched by the blood of the workmen which it can shed unpunished."

On the 31st of the same month, three Indians were extracted, suffocated, from the Central Shaft; of whom only one showed signs of life, and were conveyed, as I am told, at ten o'clock in the morning, on a cart, to the Company's hospital. And what of the authorities? The authorities do not know whether some accident has caused these victims.

The commands of the Labour Act, like those of any other Peruvian law, are not minded in the least by the Company. Another victim of the kind, the labourer Cirilo Sosa, assistant electrician at the foundry of "Smelter", was invalidated by an accident which happened on 6th March, and has not received until now the due indemnization.

It is impossible that such attentates should continue with inpunity. For this reason I denounce them to Your Excellency, in the hope that this time they will receive the necessary penal sanction. As the United States believe to day that they have a right to intervene in analogous affairs happening at the Putumayo and send a commissioner to that region, it behoves Your Excellency to execute justice on the crimes which the North-American citizens commit at Cerro de Pasco, thus insinuating that the duty of that Republic does not lie so much in the far-away forests of the Oriental region, but rather here, in the Cerro de Pasco, where its citizens do not appear as heralds of civilization.

For the said reasons I ask Your Excellency to attend to my demand. It is just etc."

Your Excellency.'"

NOTES.

(A page 7)

This measurement is not uniformly the same in all cases, but with respect to our purpose it suffices to know what amount of money the Company pays for the number of "pertenencias" it owns and the quantity of ore drawn from its possessions.

(B page 9)

An official note addressed by the Major of the Town Council of Cerro de Pasco to the Prefect of the Department of Junin:

Cerro, August 3d 1908.

To the Prefect of the Department:

By agreement of the Council which I preside, taken at the session of 23d July last, I have the honour to address myself to Your Honour that at Smelter exists a general provision store, called the Mercantile, and that this commercial house has issued a strange currency, under the name of "fichas", which are discounted at an arbitrary avaluation by the same.

As alterations in the national money can only be made by Sorereign Congress, and as every kind of money which is not coined by express law, must be considered as false, the circulation of those "fichas", in that place is illegal, to the most serious damage of the large number of workmen who are employed at the said office.

Considering therefore the importance of this affair, the Honourable Town Council hopes that Your Honour will give to it a preferent attention, so as to avoid the circulation of the false money.

I take advantage of this opportunity to repeat to Your Honour the expressions of my high regard.

God preserve Your Honour.

Juan Azalía.

(C page 14)

A respectable engineer comments the preceding paragraphs saying that the mining excavations under towns like Saint Etiennce, Virginia etc., produce, even when well timbered, inevitable depressions of the ground, and adds that at Cerro de Pasco, these excavations being effected from below towards the surface, from the new zone towards the old one, which has been shaken by three centuries of work badly done, result even more inevitable. Therefore, instead of protesting against the works which are undertaken to withdraw the metal from this rich zone, steps should rather be taken to insure equitable indemnizations for the owners of the endangered properties.

The Corps of Mining Engineers formulated a project tending to fix proper rules for the exploitation and inspection of the works, which remained unheeded however amongst the papers of the Superior Mining Council, only being published in N° 33 and following of the Bulletin of the Corps of Mining Engineers and serving Government to extract from it some convenient articles on occasion of the catastrophe of Gollarisquisga, mentioned in the former pages of this pamphlet.

(D page 27)

Art. 12 of the by-law about the contracts of services for the mining industry (4th September 1903):

In case that a labourer should lose his life or incapacitate himself for work through some accident that might happen, and which could not be imputed to the way in which he executed his task, the owner of the industry must pay to that labourer or his children who are under age, or his widow, the indemnization which has been stipulated in the contract. In default of a special pact, the Deputation must fix a pension according to its judgment, which do not exceed half of the salary, for a term of two or three years, without this preventing that the persons concerned, who be not satisfied with this arrangement, apply to the Common Judge.

(E page 29)

Decree which regulates the proceeding which shall be observed in the exploitation of coal-mines.

The President of the Republic

Considering that

The progress and development of the exploitation of coal-mines makes necessary the adoption of measures which may impede as much as possible the unfortunate accidents which are happening there,

Decrees:

Art. 1.—In every coal mine it is prohibited to enter with, or have there in use, lamps whose light is in contact with the air and which be not security-lamps. It is also prohibited to open the lamp, smoke, light a match etc.;

Art. 2.—All the diggings of a coal mine must have a width of at least two metres and have a sufficient current of air to make sure the sweeping away of the gases;

Art. 3.—The old mines which are not in use and the abandoned ones must be conveniently closed to avoid the access of air;

Art. 4.—In every place where works are executed, a security-lamp must be kept hanging from the ceiling and near to it, so that the presence of grisu may be betrayed by the diminution of the light;

Art. 5.—The lower perforations must not be executed in a parallel direction, or with their mouth inclined towards the ground, so as to avoid that by the commotion of a shot be caused an explosion of the coal-dust;

Art. 6.—The shots must be let off by electricity or with security matches long enough to leave the labourers time to retire from the wall at a distance of over a hundred metres, the matches having to be lighted with safety-tinders;

Art. 7.—In every coal-mine it is prohibited that any person, except those especially charged with the task, should fire the shots, it being requisite that one particular gang be dedicated to this purpose in each watch;

Art. 8.—It is prohibited to use black powder in the coal-mine and other than safety-explosives;

Art. 9.—In all the coal-mines must be provided, besides the general maps of the mine, a special one in which the direction of the currents of air be indicated, these having to be also indicated in the mine itself;

Art. 10.—Every coal-mine must be provided with all the necessary material to equip, at least, four gangs of rescuers, composed of five men each;

Art. 11.—In every coal-mine must be provided places of retreat for the workers and these be disinfected frequently by the process of extractuntilicio;

Art. 12.—In every coal-mine must be provided printed instructions which advise the danger, the way of avoiding it and the means of rescue, once the accident has been produced, and these, besides being distributed to the captains of the mine and the labourers, must be fixed in the visible places within the mine and be revised by the Delegate and the appointed skilled superviser;

Art. 13.—In every coal-mine must be appointed one or more persons, according to the importance of the exploitation, who at the relief of each watch examine all the works of the mine, to see whether grisu has formed, burning the air and taking samples of the same, for analization;

Art. 14.—All the above measures must be introduced in every coal-mine within a term that shall not exceed four months;

Art. 15.—Only those mines may continue to be worked immediately, which according to the opinion of the Delegates do not offer danger to the lives of the labourers.

Issued at Government House, Lima, on the twentyeigth of the month of January nineteenhundred ten.

Ego Aguirre.   *A. B. Leguía.*

(F page 45)

We will cite the case of an anonymous victim who perished at Smelter, about three years ago.

The misfortune was witnessed by several artizans employed on the spot, although they did not think of noting down either the name or the date which it would have been interesting to know. Things happened thus: in the large convertors, where the copper is smelted, the excess of heat makes the clay crumble away from the sides, and a foreman had the temerity to order an Indian labourer to clean away the remnants of clay from the convertor, the man dying instantaneously fron asfixiation, when he obeyed the bidding. We are told that upon many occasions the workmen are obliged to go near similar deposits, whilst these are still too hot to be approached, at an imminent risk of their lives, all this owing to the reckless hurry of the foremen in carrying on the operations.

[

U.C. BERKELEY LIBRARIES

C006428460

RETURN TO ➡

1	2	3
4	5	6

ALL BOOKS MAY BE RECALLED AFTER 7 DAYS

DUE AS STAMPED BELOW

LIBRARY USE ONLY
NOV 2 6 1997
CIRCULATION DEPT.

JUL 0 7 1999

FORM NO. DD 19

UNIVERSITY OF CALIFORNIA, BERKELEY
BERKELEY, CA 94720

CPSIA information can be obtained
at www.ICGtesting.com
Printed in the USA
BVHW041710031218
534659BV00016B/792/P